Remnant Children, Children's Book

Written by: Neisha A. Sibley

Dedication

I dedicate this book to every child who is set apart and called by God.

This book belongs to

Date

WE ARE REMNANT CHIDLREN

Remnant children are children who are set apart and called by God. Remnant children may not always have the same interests as other children. Remnant Children are:

- Gifted
- Prayerful
- Brave and Bold
- Obedient

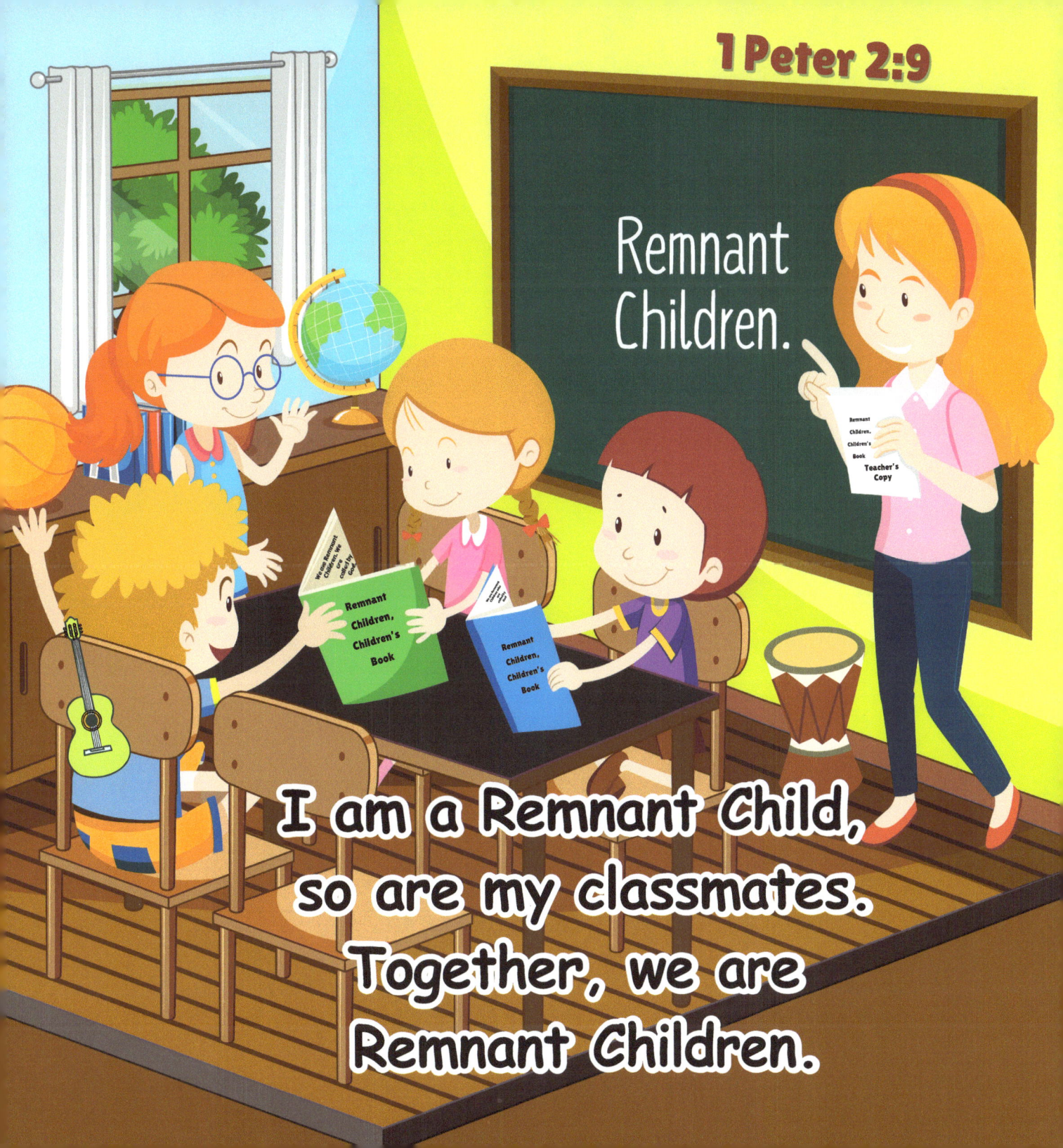

1 Peter 2:9

Remnant Children.

I am a Remnant Child, so are my classmates. Together, we are Remnant Children.

"I am a Remnant Child and I love to sing. God has given me a beautiful voice, so I will use it to glorify Him."
-Prov 18:16

REMNANT

"I can do all things through Christ which strengtheneth me." –Phil 4:13

"I am a Remnant Child and I love to paint. Painting makes me happy!"

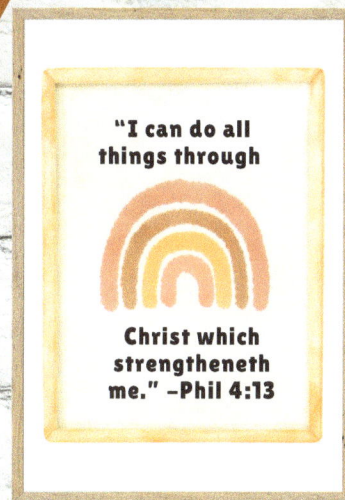

My gifts are not just for me. God has given me these gifts to bring Him glory.

MENU

Everyone has a talent. Some people have more than one talent. God has given us so many great talents and gifts that make us unique in our own way. Do you know what your talent is?

" We love to bake. Baking is our talent. One day we will bake a lot of cookies to help feed the homeless."

"My friend and I get so much joy from growing crops in our garden. The seeds we planted are already producing. Look! "

FARM

"Thank you Jesus for giving us this wonderful talent!
One day we will have a big farm so that we can donate food all across the world."

What is your talent?
Can you identify it below?

 **Cooking/baking**  **Painting**  **Playing music Singing**

 **Making crafts**  **Dancing**  **Playing sports**  **Writing**

 **Reading**  **Photography**  **Fixing/building**  **Gardening**

One way to identify your talent is to think about something that you can do very well.

Cooking/baking   Painting   Playing music   Singing

Making crafts   Dancing   Playing sports   Writing

Reading   Photography   Fixing/building   Gardening

If your talent is not shown above, you can draw a picture of your talent or talents in the box below.

Remnant Children are Praying Children

"But Jesus said, 'Let the little children come to me. Don't stop them, because the kingdom of heaven belongs to people who are like these children.'"

–Matt 19:14

Remnant Children

PRAY

Remnant children pray over their food

Remnant Children
are not too young
to hear
the voice of God.
1 Sam 3

In the bible, the Lord spoke to a young boy named Samuel. At first, Samuel thought that someone else was calling him but it was God calling young Samuel. Samuel listened to hear what God was saying. Like Samuel, Remnant children can hear the voice of God too.

Remnant Children are not too young to hear the voice of God.
1 Sam 3
Dear God thank You for giving me a great day today. Thank You for protecting me and my friends. Please protect mom and dad on their way home. Amen.
Prayer is not only asking God for things, but also praising Him for His goodness each and every day.

Remnant Children
are not too young
to hear
the voice of God.

1 Sam 3

"When I pray, I communicate with God and tell Him all about my day. And when I am done talking, I must listen to hear what He has to say."

Remnant Children are Brave and Bold

Joshua 1 : 9

In the bible, the Lord commanded Joshua to be brave and not to be afraid. Like Joshua, I can be brave too because God is with me.

"I am brave and bold. I will not shy away from what God has called me to do. God is with me so I will not be afraid."

"For God did not give us a spirit that makes us afraid. He gave us a spirit of power, and love and self-control."
2 Tim 1:7

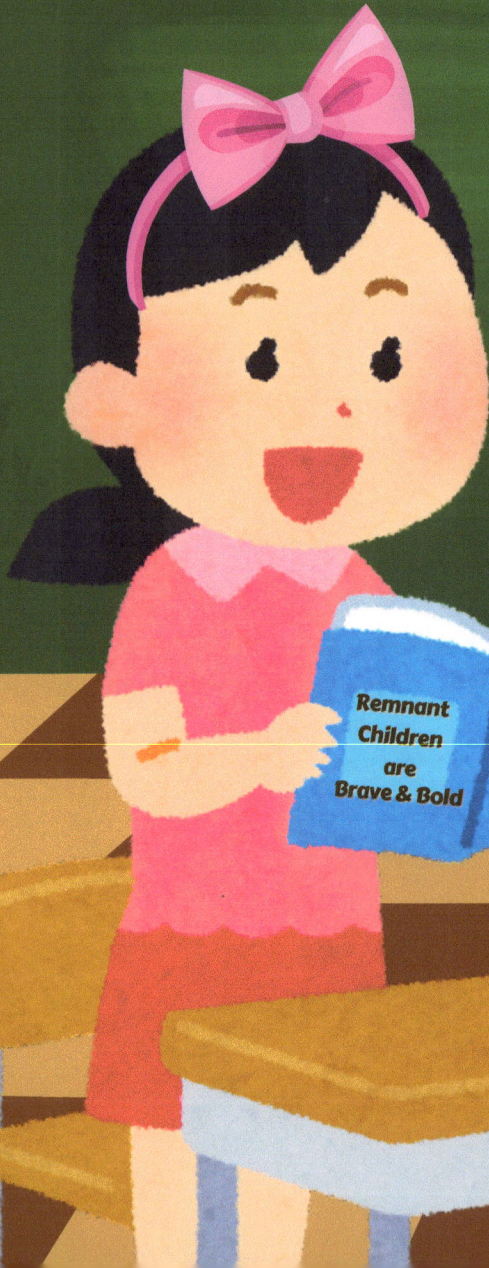

When my teacher asks me to read aloud, I will be happy to do it because I am brave and bold. I will not get nervous or cry. God is with me at all times so I don't need to be afraid. Even if I make a mistake, that is okay because I will learn from it so that I can do better next time.

Remnant Children are Obedient.

EPHESIANS 6:1

"Children, obey your parents in the Lord: for this is right."

God has given parents the responsibility of keeping children safe at all times. When children obey their parents, they are following God's rules and God will be happy with their lives.

Remnant Children Make Good Choices Out of Obedience.

"My mom said I should eat my vegetables first, then ice-cream later. I want to be obedient, so I will eat my vegetables first, and my Ice-cream later!"

Remnant Children Follow Class Instructions.

Class rules

- ☐ Teeth are for chewing food. We do not bite our friends.
- ☐ We use our kind words, we do not yell at our friends.
- ☐ We use gentle hands, we do not hurt our friends.
- ☐ We use common courtesies such as , Please, Thank You, Excuse me, I'm sorry.

Following instructions is a way of showing obedience.

Like parents, teachers are also given the responsibility of keeping children safe at all times. When children listen and obey their teachers, they will be safe from harm and danger.

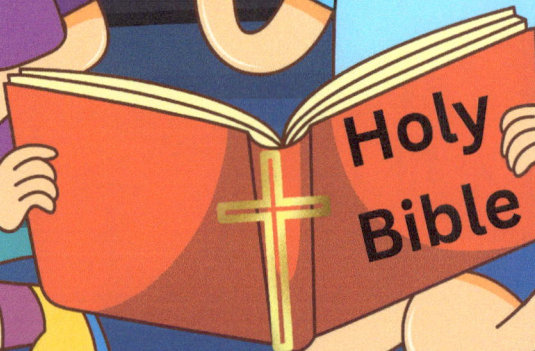

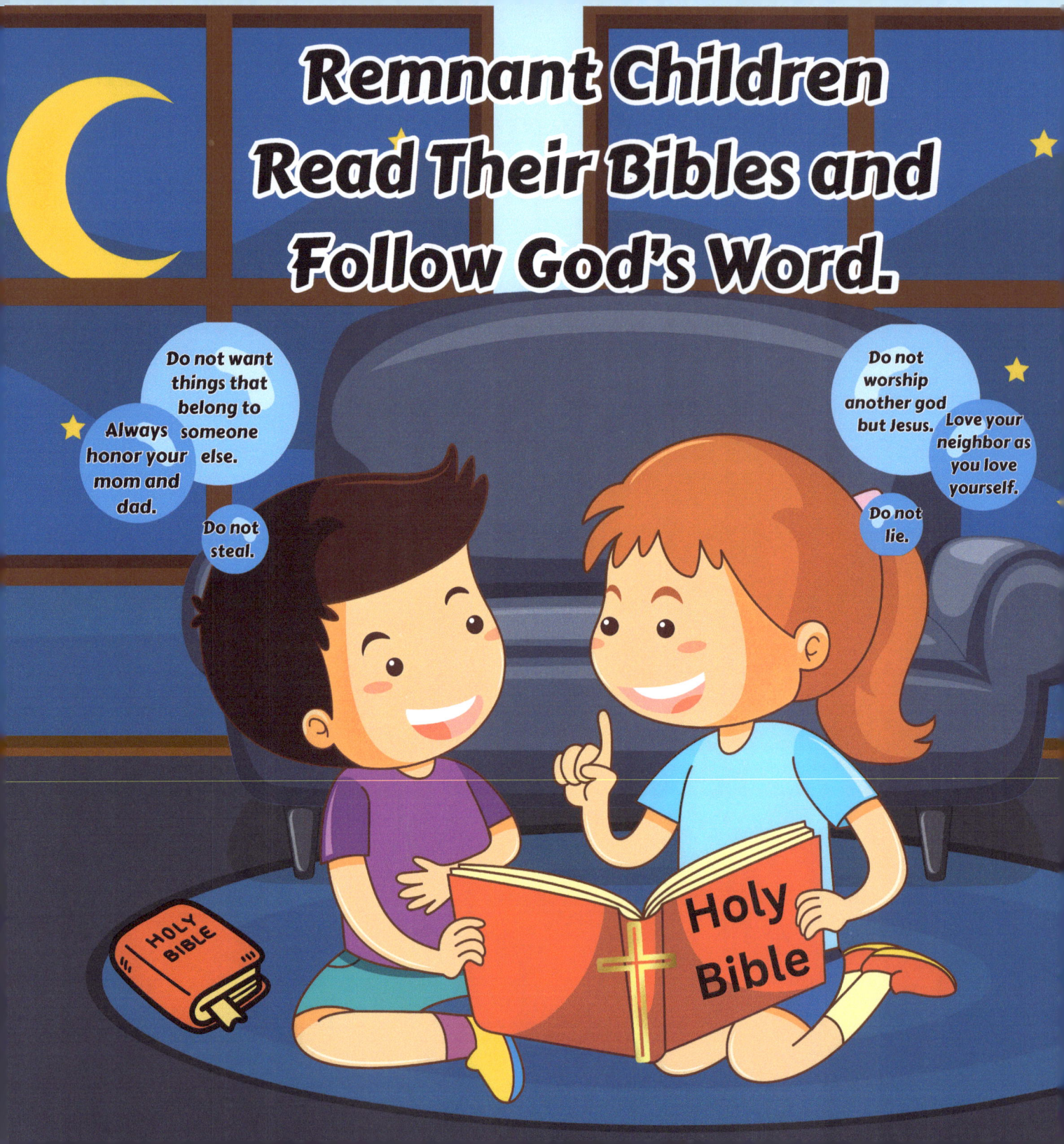

GIFTED

PRAYERFUL

BRAVE & BOLD

OBEDIENT

WE ARE REMNANT CHILDREN! WE WILL FOLLOW THE RULES IN THE BIBLE AND DO WHAT IT SAYS. REMNANT CHILDREN ARE GIFTED, PRAYERFUL, BRAVE & BOLD AND OBEDIENT. YAAY!

www.ingramcontent.com/pod-product-compliance
Lightning Source LLC
LaVergne TN
LVHW072059070426
835508LV00002B/182